D0931414

FIELD HOCKEY

Jennifer Hurtig

WEIGL PUBLISHERS INC.

Published by Weigl Publishers Inc.
350 5th Avenue, Suite 3304, PMB 6G
New York, NY 10118-0069

Editor
Frances Purslow

Cover and page design
Terry Paulhus

Library of Congress Cataloging-in-Publication Data

Hurtig, Jennifer.
   For the love of field hockey / By Jennifer Hurtig.
   p. cm. — (For the love of sports)
   Includes index.
   ISBN 1-59036-400-7 (hard cover : alk. paper) —
   ISBN 1-59036-401-5 (soft cover)
  1. Field hockey—Juvenile literature. I. Title. II. Series.
GV1017.H7H87 2007   796.355—dc22   2005028001

Printed in the United States of America

1 2 3 4 5 6 7 8 9 10 09 08 07 06

Cover: Jessica Arrold of Australia (left) and Ko Woon Oh
of Korea battle over possession of the ball during the 2004
Summer Olympic Games in Athens, Greece.

Photograph Credits
Wisconsin Historical Society (9017): page 4.

Contents

All about Field Hockey

Field hockey is an ancient team sport. It dates back more than 4,000 years. In a tomb in Egypt, scientists have found very old drawings of men playing field hockey. There is also evidence of other ancient peoples, including American Indians, playing this game long ago. In the past, it was played only by men. Today it is played by males and females of all ages.

American Indians played an earlier version of field hockey with sticks made from animal bones and balls made from deerskin.

The first men's field hockey club was formed in England in 1849. It was called Blackheath. In 1886, the Hockey Association was formed in London. The following year, the first women's field hockey club began in England. The All England Women's Hockey Association was created in 1889. The sport quickly became popular among women. Then in 1902, Constance Applebee, a gym teacher, introduced field hockey to the United States.

Today, field hockey is an Olympic sport. From 1908 to 1980, only men's field hockey teams took part in the Olympics. Then in 1980, women's field hockey was added.

The word hockey probably comes from the French word *hoquet*, which means shepherd's stick.

CHECK IT OUT

Learn more about the history of field hockey at **www.hickoksports.com/**

Click on History, then Index by Sport.

Getting Started

The object of field hockey is to score more goals than the opposite team. To do this, players use sticks to move the ball toward the goal.

Uniform shirts have numbers on the front and back.

Mouthguards are worn to protect a player's teeth from flying balls or high sticks.

As field hockey is played with sticks players wear shin guards. They are made of plastic, fiberglass, or rubber. They protect lower legs from injury.

Long socks match the team's colors. Socks hold shin guards in place. They help the **umpire** see the different teams.

Sticks are made of wood or a fiberglass mixture. They weigh between 16 and 24 ounces (450 and 680 grams). Sticks vary in length from 26 to 38 inches (66 to 96 centimeters.) Only the front of a field hockey stick is flat. The "toe" or "head" of the stick curves upward.

Most field hockey balls are made of plastic. These balls are usually white, but can also be yellow or orange. They weigh about 5.5 ounces (156 g).

Female players often wear skirts, and males wear shorts.

For outdoor games, players wear cleats to grip the grass. At higher levels of play, they wear **turf shoes** because they play on artificial turf. Shoes with soft soles are worn for indoor games.

The Playing Field

Field hockey is played both indoors and outdoors. It is mainly played outdoors around the world. However, indoor field hockey is played in some countries when weather prevents playing outside during part of the year.

An outdoor field is about twice the size of an indoor field. Outdoor fields measure 100 yards (91.4 meters) long by 60 yards (55 m) wide. Both indoor and outdoor fields have goal cages. Outdoor goal cages are 7 feet (2.1 m) high and 12 feet (3.7 m) wide. Indoor cages are smaller. Both fields are marked with centerlines and **striking circles**. Outdoor fields also have a 25-yard (23 m) line on each half.

Olympic field hockey is played outdoors without sideboards. Athletes must fight to keep the ball within bounds.

One main difference between the two types of fields is that indoor fields have sideboards. In outdoor field hockey, the ball can go out of bounds by crossing the **sideline**. When played indoors, the ball rebounds off the boards and stays in play.

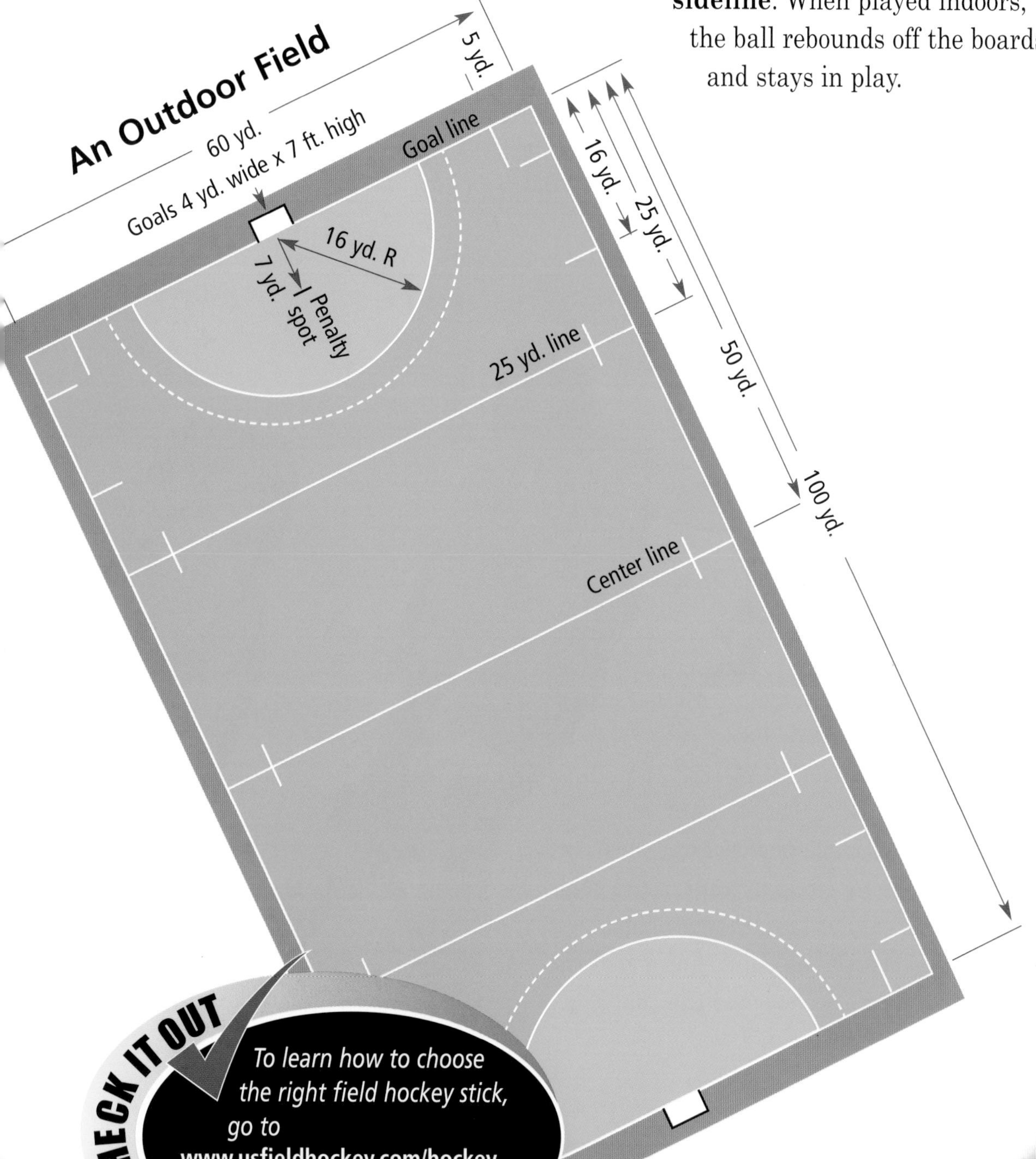

An Outdoor Field

60 yd.

5 yd.

Goals 4 yd. wide x 7 ft. high

Goal line

16 yd. R

7 yd. spot | Penalty

16 yd.

25 yd.

50 yd.

100 yd.

25 yd. line

Center line

CHECK IT OUT

To learn how to choose the right field hockey stick, go to **www.usfieldhockey.com/hockey**

Then click on Equipment.

Rules of the Game

Before the beginning of a game, the umpire flips a coin. The winner of the coin toss stands in the center of the field facing the ball. At the whistle, the player hits the ball to a teammate. This is called a pass back. At the beginning of the second half, the other team does the pass back. Pass backs also occur at the center of the field after every goal.

Players may only play the ball with the face, or flat part, of the stick.

The aim of field hockey is to score as many goals as possible. Players use their sticks to **dribble** or pass the ball up the field to their teammates. While the players are moving the ball up the field toward the goal, the other team tries to gain possession of the ball. The player who has the ball cannot shield the ball with his or her body. This is against the rules and is called obstruction. Once inside the striking circle in front of the goal cage, the ball carrier tries to score a goal. Every goal is worth one point. For a goal to count, the ball must pass over the goal line between the goalposts.

When players lift the curled edge of their sticks above their shoulders, hit the ball with their hands, or use their body to stop the ball, a **foul** is called. **Stick interference** is also a foul. When a foul occurs within the striking circle, the umpire awards the opposite team a **penalty corner** or **penalty stroke**.

In outdoor field hockey, each team has 10 players on the field in addition to the goalie. At the high school level, games are divided into two periods of 30 minutes each. There is a 5-minute break between the halves. For college and international level games, each half runs for 35 minutes with a 10-minute break.

In indoor field hockey, each team has five players and a goalie. The game has two 20-minute periods.

Umpires call penalties for dangerous play and bad behavior.

CHECK IT OUT

Learn more about field hockey rules at **www.wikipedia.org**. Type "Field Hockey" into the Search field.

Positions on the Field

In field hockey, offensive players dribble or pass the ball forward and then try to score goals. Other players on the team defend their goal and try to take the ball from the attackers on the other team.

Forwards play on the front line and attack the other team. Sometimes a coach puts five players on the forward line, and sometimes only three. A center forward plays in the middle of two wings in the front line. The two wings are the right wing and the left wing. Wings are also called outside-forwards. They help take the ball to the opposing side of the field and pass the ball to the center. When there are five players on the front line, the people in between the wings and centers are called inners. The front line players all work together passing the ball back and forth. They also try to find ways to shoot and score on the opposing net.

For penalty corners, play is stopped to allow teams to take their positions. The attacking team must stand outside the striking circle. One attacker stands on the back line and passes the ball to his or her teammates.

Players called halfbacks, links, or midfielders play on the middle line. Players in this position have two key roles. They help their defense tackle **opponents**. They also pass the ball to the forward line.

Defenders play on the back line and are called fullbacks or backs. They help clear the ball from their goal area and attack the forwards on the opposite team. One of the backs is chosen as a sweeper. The sweeper plays right in front of the goalie and helps defend the net. The sweeper helps block shots and **intercepts** the other team's plays.

The goalie is the only player who can kick the ball.

Goalies block attackers' shots with their body, gloves, leg pads, and stick. They are not allowed to catch the ball. The goalie's jersey is a different color from the players on the field.

Championships

In North America, most field hockey players are female, but there are some men's teams as well. In some countries, such as India, Pakistan, the Netherlands, Germany, and Australia, field hockey is very popular among males.

Field hockey is played by all ages. Elementary schools and high schools often have junior teams. Many colleges and universities also have field hockey teams. They compete in intercollegiate tournaments and sometimes travel to other countries to compete. National teams play in tournaments around the world.

India has won eight Olympic gold medals for field hockey. They have won more gold medals than any other country.

CHECK IT OUT

Find out more about U.S. field hockey events at

www.usfieldhockey.com/champions

The Olympic Games and the World Cup provide national field hockey teams with the chance to become world champions. Both competitions are held every four years. Twelve men's field hockey teams and 10 women's teams compete in the Olympics. The top 16 men's and women's field hockey teams take part in the World Cup.

Germany won gold for women's field hockey at the 2004 Olympics in Athens, Greece. The very first Olympics were held in Greece nearly 3,000 years ago.

The United States has sent field hockey teams to the Pan American Games since the sport was first added to the men's program in 1967 and the women's program 20 years later. The Pan Am Games are always held the summer before the Olympics.

The Champions Trophy Cup is a key field hockey tournament played every year. The six top teams in the world compete. The Commonwealth Games, the FIH Junior World Cup, and the U.S. Field Hockey National Hockey Festival are also key events. In the off-season, the National Indoor Tournament is the main event for U.S. field hockey players.

Pioneers of the Sport

Field hockey attracts many types of athletes. Some prefer to play at the local club level, while others aim for international competition.

BETH ANDERS

POSITION
Midfield
TEAM
U.S. World Cup Team
COUNTRY
United States
DATE OF BIRTH
November 13, 1951

Career Facts:

- Beth scored three goals to help the United States Women's Field Hockey team win the Four Nations Cup in 1983.
- Some of Beth's shots were as fast as 75 miles (127 km) per hour.
- Beth was the first woman to be named Top Amateur Athlete by the Philadelphia Sports Writers' Association.

ALYSON ANNAN

POSITION
Forward
TEAM
Balsam Pacific Arrows
COUNTRY
Australia
DATE OF BIRTH
June 21, 1973

Career Facts:

- In 1998, Alyson became the first person to be named International Hockey Federation's Player of the Year.
- As a member of the Hockeyroos team, Alyson won gold medals in the 1996 and 2000 Olympics.
- By 2001, Alyson scored 149 goals in 201 international games.

TEUN DE NOOIJER

POSITION
Forward
TEAM
Dutch National Team
COUNTRY
Holland
DATE OF BIRTH
March 22, 1976

Career Facts:

- Teun won World Player of the Year in 2003.
- He won gold as a member of the Dutch National Team in the 1996 and 2000 Olympic Games.
- Teun is also a double World Cup winner. He won in 1998 and in 2002.

ANNE TOWNSEND

POSITION
Halfback and fullback
TEAM
All-American
COUNTRY
United States
DATE OF BIRTH
1900

Career Facts:

- Anne was president of the U.S. Field Hockey Association from 1928 to 1932.
- She was team captain for the All-American team from 1924 to 1938, except for 1933.
- After a break from field hockey, Anne rejoined the All-American team when she was 47 years old.

Superstars of the Game

Field hockey heroes of today inspire young athletes to try this exciting sport.

LUCIANA AYMAR

POSITION
Midfield
TEAM
Jockey Club Rosario
COUNTRY
Argentina
DATE OF BIRTH
August 10, 1977

Career Facts:

- Luciana was named International Hockey Federation (FIH) Player of the Year in 2001 and 2004.
- She played on the team that won the 1999 Pan American Games.
- Her team also won a silver medal at the 2000 Olympics in Sydney, Australia.

MIKE MAHOOD

POSITION
Goalkeeper
TEAM
Canadian National Team
COUNTRY
Canada
DATE OF BIRTH
November 11, 1975

Career Facts:

- Mike played in the 1998 World Cup in the Netherlands.
- Mike was goalkeeping in the 1999 victory over Argentina during the Pan American Games in Canada.
- His team placed second in the 2000 Americas Cup in Cuba.

KATE BARBER

POSITION
Forward/Midfield
TEAM
USA National Team
COUNTRY
United States
DATE OF BIRTH
November 22, 1976

Career Facts:

- Kate was named USA Field Hockey Athlete of the Year in 2002 and 2004.
- She played in the 2002 World Cup in Perth, Australia.
- Kate's team won silver medals in both the 1999 Pan American Games and the 2001 Americas Cup.

GRANT SCHUBERT

POSITION
Forward
TEAM
Adelaide Hotshots
COUNTRY
Australia
DATE OF BIRTH
August 1, 1980

Career Facts:

- Grant won a gold medal in the 2004 Olympic Games in Athens, Greece.
- He was named the World Hockey Young Player of the Year in 2003.
- Grant scored nine goals in six matches in the 2003 Champions Trophy tournament. He was the second highest goal scorer.

CHECK IT OUT

To see photos of international field hockey events, go to **www.fihockey.org**

Then click on Photo Gallery and select an event.

Staying Healthy

Field hockey is a fast-paced sport. Players need to be in top condition to perform well. Drinking plenty of water before, during, and after field hockey games is important. Players lose water from their bodies when they sweat during a game. That water needs to be replaced.

Eating healthy foods from all four food groups keeps field hockey players strong and full of energy. Grain products, fruits, and vegetables provide vitamins, minerals, and fiber for an athlete's body. Calcium in dairy products keeps bones strong. Meat, eggs, and other sources of protein build muscle.

It is important to eat 5 to 9 servings of vegetables a day. A big salad can count for 2 to 4 servings.

CHECK IT OUT

Learn more about how to prepare your body to play sports at

http://health.yahoo.com/ centers/fitness/5

Lifting weights strengthens an athlete's arm muscles.

To stretch your leg muscles, slowly try to touch your toes.

Good field hockey players have speed, strength, and skill. **Conditioning** is important before, during, and after the game. It helps players breathe easier, avoid injuries, and run faster. Different kinds of conditioning include stretching, weight training, **cardiovascular training**, and **agility training**.

Players stretch before and after practices and games. This helps prepare them for running and helps reduce injuries. Many parts of the body should be stretched. This includes the legs, ankles, back, arms, shoulders, and neck.

Cardiovascular training, such as jogging and bicycling, help strengthen a player's heart and lungs. This is important because field hockey involves much running. Weight training builds strong muscles. Strong muscles help players hit the ball hard and run fast. Agility training improves a player's ball control and speed.

Field Hockey Brain Teasers

Test your field hockey knowledge by answering these brain teasers!

Q How old is the game of field hockey?

A Field hockey dates back more than 4,000 years.

Q Are field hockey players allowed to kick the ball?

A No, only goalies are allowed to kick the ball.

Q Which player helps the goalie defend the goal cage?

A The sweeper helps the goalie.

Q Is field hockey only played outdoors?

A In some countries, field hockey is also played indoors.

Q What is it called when players try to shield the ball with their bodies?

A It is called obstruction.

Q What happens when a foul is called?

A The other team is awarded a penalty corner or penalty shot.

Glossary

agility training: training that improves speed

cardiovascular training: training that improves breathing and heart rate

conditioning: exercising and eating well to make the body fit

dribble: control the ball with the stick while running down the field

foul: behavior that is against the rules

intercepts: stops a player and takes the ball away

opponents: players on the opposite team

penalty corner: a free shot at the other team's goal taken from outside the striking circle. Several teammates on both teams are involved in the play.

penalty stroke: a free shot at the other team's goal taken from at least 7 yards (6.4 m) out; only the goalie and the shooter take part

sideline: a line that runs along the borders of the field

stick interference: a foul called when a player brings his or her stick in contact with another player's stick

striking circles: semi-circles on the field in front of the goal cages

turf shoes: athletic shoes with rubber bumps on the bottom for gripping artificial turf

umpire: a person who enforces the rules of the game

Index